Modern Art

PAULINE RIDLEY

Thomson Learning
New York

ART AND ARTISTS

Ancient Art
Art in the Nineteenth Century
Impressionism
Modern Art
Renaissance Art
Western Art 1600-1800

Cover *Moon Woman* by Jackson Pollock.
Museum of Modern Art, New York.

Title page *The Scream* by Edvard Munch.
National Gallery of Norway, Oslo.

First published in the
United States in 1995 by
Thomson Learning
New York, NY

Published simultaneously in Great Britain by
Wayland (Publishers) Limited

U.K. version copyright © 1995 Wayland (Publishers) Ltd.

U.S. version copyright © 1995 Thomson Learning

Library of Congress Cataloging-in-Publication Data
Ridley, Pauline.
  Modern art / Pauline Ridley.
      p.   cm.—(Art and artists)
  Includes bibliographical references and index.
  Summary: An illustrated survey of twentieth-century
modern art, from Matisse to such recent artists as Paula
Rego and Anthony Gormley.
  ISBN 1-56847-356-7
  1. Art, Modern—20th century—Juvenile literature.
[1. Art, Modern—20th century. 2. Art appreciation.]
I. Title. II. Series: Art and artists (Thomson Learning
(Firm))
N6490.R542   1995
701'.1--dc20   95-1963

Printed in Italy

Picture acknowledgments

The photographs in this book were supplied by: AKG London 8 (left), 11, 16, 29 (right), 39 (left); Bridgeman Art Library *cover* (main and background pictures), 5, 6, 7, 8 (right), 9 (right) 14, 15 (left), 17 (right), 18, 19 (both), 20, 21, (right), 23, 24, 25 (left), 27, 28, 30, 31, 32–33, 34 (both), 35, 37, 40, 41 (left); British Museum 10; Christies Colour Library 21 (left), 22; Eye Ubiquitous 4; E.T. Archive 26; Heydt Museum 13; National Gallery, Oslo 9 (left); Tate Gallery (London), 15 (right), 41 (right), 43 (right), 45 (left); Tate Gallery (Liverpool) 45 (right); Topham Picture Library 39 (right); Visual Arts Library 12, 17 (left), 25 (right), 36, 44; Waddington Gallery 38; Women's Slide Library 29 (left). The photographs of works on pages 42 and 43 (left) were kindly supplied by the artists.

The following works are reproduced with the permission of the copyright holders: © ADAGP, Paris and DACS, London 1995: Constantin Brancusi *Sleeping Muse* (1910) p.17, Georges Braque *Clarinet and Bottle of Rum* (1911) p.15, Robert Delaunay *Homage to Blériot* (1914) p.17, Sonia Delaunay *Design for Clothes and Citroën* (1925) p.25, André Derain *Charing Cross Bridge* (1906) p.8, Marcel Duchamp *Bride Stripped Bare by her Bachelors. Even* (1923) p.19, Alberto Giacometti *Painted Bronze* (1950) p.36, Natalia Gontcharova *Le Coq d'Or* (1914) p.20, Arshile Gorky *The Waterfall* (1943) p.34, Wassily Kandinsky *Cossacks* (1910) p.12, René Magritte *The Human Condition II* (1935) p.29, Joan Miró *Head of a Catalan Peasant* (1925) p.26; © ARS, NY and DACS, London 1995: – Willem de Kooning *Woman I* (1952) p.35, Mark Rothko *Red on Maroon* (1959) p.37, Frank Stella *Hyena Stomp* (1962) p.41; © DACS, London 1995:– Jean Arp *The Forest* (1916) p.19, Giorgio de Chirico *Italian Piazza: Melancholy* (1912) p.28, Fernand Léger *The Mechanic* (1920) p.23, Jules Grun *Friday at the French Artist's Salon* (1911) p.6, Hannah Höch *Priestess* (1934) p.22, Paul Klee *They're Biting* (1920) p.25, Meret Oppenheim *Fur Breakfast* (1936) p.29, Pablo Picasso *Les Demoiselles d'Avignon* (1907) p.14, *Still Life* (1914) p.15, *Guernica* (1937) pp. 32–33, Paul Signac *St. Tropez* (1905) p.5; © David Smith/DACS, London/VAGA, New York 1995 David Smith *Cubi XVIII* (1964) p.40; Robert Rauschenberg/DACS, London/VAGA, New York 1995 Robert Rauschenberg *Retroactive II* (1964) p.39; © 1995 ABC/Mondrian Estate/Holtzman Trust. by ILP – Piet Mondrian *Composition with Red, Yellow and Blue* (1937) p.24; © Succession H. Matisse/DACS 1995 *Open Window, Collioure* (1905) p.7, *Goldfish* (1911) p.8.

Copyright permission has been sought for all works still in copyright, but in some instances it has been unobtainable. The publishers apologize for any omissions.

CONTENTS

1 INTRODUCTION

Mythological Illustration by Michael Tommy Tjarbarudi. People often ask what modern art means, as though there were a secret code to help them read a hidden message. But the meaning of all kinds of art changes in different situations. For instance, the patterns in Australian aboriginal bark paintings originally symbolized a sacred connection between people and land; now they are found on T-shirts promoting the tourist industry or hung in art galleries like abstract paintings. But these works can also help teach people something about their makers' lives and beliefs. When young Australian aboriginal artists use these dot patterns today, they are drawing on *all* those meanings to explore their heritage and their place in modern Australia.

Some of the work discussed in this book was made around the turn of the century. So why is it still called "modern" art? Cars and planes made in the early 1900s seem very old-fashioned now, because people expect them to change. But people sometimes assume that art should always stay the same, describing the world in the same ways.

If you look at other books in this series, you will see that the word "art" is used to describe many different types of object – masks and pots, paintings, and statues. They have different jobs to do, such as decorating people's homes, telling stories, recording the appearance of people and places, or playing parts in religious ceremonies.

In the fifteenth century, artists developed new ways of representing the world to help them to tell religious stories as vividly as possible. The same techniques were used to record what people looked like, but the invention of photography in the nineteenth century made this less important. By then, everyday life was changing. More people lived in cities, and new technology was speeding up travel and communication. Each generation was very conscious that modern life was different from their parents' experience.

St. Tropez by Paul Signac (1863–1935). These dots have a different purpose to the pattern in the bark painting. They reflect an interest in scientific color theory as well as the surface pattern of a painting. Work such as this bridged impressionist art and Matisse's early work. *Musée des Beaux Arts, Grenoble, France*.

Some people wanted art to show those changes; others preferred to stick to familiar ways of seeing the world. Later in this book you will see that arguments about what art should look like are usually connected to disagreements about what it is for.

Traditional "realistic" painting was a skill that almost anyone could be taught, but now when very few people learn it, it can seem like magic. In addition, many people still feel annoyed or disappointed by things that are different, especially art that is abstract – that is, art that isn't a copy of the appearance of the world around us.

Liking one type of music, however, does not keep people from enjoying other types, and it would be a shame if people who admired traditional skills make us close our eyes and minds to other forms of visual expression. Painting and sculpture (and all kinds of video and performance art that cannot be shown well in books) can deal with ideas and feelings that are impossible to express in words or music. Throughout our lives we are surrounded by images that can affect the way we feel about ourselves. Art can help us to explore this part of our lives.

2 MATISSE AND FAUVISM

In the past, artists earned their livings by making paintings and sculptures ordered by people who wanted them. By the beginning of the twentieth century, however, most artists worked without a particular customer in mind. In Europe, they would try to get their work shown at one of the big art exhibitions that were held every year, called Salons. They hoped to attract the attention of the art critics who wrote for the newspapers, trusting that the publicity would encourage someone to buy. It was similar to the music or art industry today, where artists try to get their work reviewed by the media so people will know about their art and buy it.

At the time of the Salons, artists and critics were beginning to talk less about what was pictured in a painting (its subject) and more about the technique, or how it was painted.

One technique, from the fifteenth century, is called perspective. The word comes from a French word that means "looking through." It is used to make an image on a flat surface look three-dimensional, as though the painting were a real scene that a person might see through a window. Perspective is the technique used when an artist makes one object, such a tree, smaller than a similar object. The smaller object will look farther away. Because of this

Left *Open Window, Collioure* by Henri Matisse (1869–1954). This is a tiny picture compared to the painting opposite, but the use of color gives it lots of energy. The boats in the harbor seem just as close as the flowerpots on the balcony, because of the way the reds and greens sizzle, pulling our eyes back to the painted surface of the picture. *John Hay Whitney Collection, New York.*

Far left *Friday at the Salon* by Jules Grun (1868–1934). The fashionable people at the official Salon seem more interested in one another than in the work on display. Many younger artists preferred to show their work at smaller independent Salons, where it could have more impact. *Musée des Beaux Arts, Rouen.*

"Isms" and Insults

Music journalists and disc jockeys often use general labels like "heavy metal" or "house music" to describe different types of sound. In the same way, critics trying to pick out new tendencies in art often invent labels like impressionism or cubism. Sometimes, a group might invent its own name, especially if the members want to get publicity; but many names started as insults in the popular press, such as when Matisse and his friends were called *"fauves"'* (wild beasts) when they showed their work.

technique, the person viewing a traditional painting will feel drawn in, or drawn through the window, by the subject, making the subject of the painting more important than the frame, the paint, or the brush strokes, which one doesn't notice as easily.

By the early twentieth century, following the example of the impressionists and post-impressionists, including Paul Cézanne (1839–1906), Georges Seurat (1859–91), and Paul Gauguin (1848–1903), many younger artists were interested in exploring a looser style, using paint in a more obvious way and with more adventurous use of color.

Left *The Goldfish Bowl* by Henri Matisse. Greens contrast vibrantly with pinks and oranges while the black helps to sharpen the design. The thinly applied paint looks casual, but the picture is carefully observed – see how the light refracts the image of the goldfish on the water surface. *Pushkin Museum, Moscow.*

Above *Charing Cross Bridge* by André Derain (1880–1954), who made several paintings of the Thames River during a visit to London. *Tate Gallery, London.*

When Henri Matisse was painting in the south of France, he found that bright sunshine can make colors look pale. But, if painted that way, they lose the feeling of heat and light. Matisse and his friends discovered that using large patches of bright color with a lot of white between them was a solution; as the patches grew, the pattern they made on the canvas became as important as the subject of the picture's composition.

When Matisse, along with Maurice de Vlaminck (1876–1958) and André Derain, showed this kind of work at the Autumn Salon in Paris in 1905, a critic called them "*fauve*s," or "wild animals." But Matisse was not trying to be shocking. In fact, he later said that he wanted his art to be like a comforting armchair that you could rest in. Some people have argued that art should be more than simply beautiful decoration for the walls of people rich enough to buy it. They believe that art should be uncomfortable because it should make people ask questions about how they see things or about social issues. Matisse, however, who had originally started painting when he was ill, believed that all people needed art to make them feel better – simple, peaceful images that raise people's spirits.

3 EXPRESSIONISM

Above *The Scream* by Edvard Munch (1863–1944). *National Gallery of Norway, Oslo.*

Right *Self-Portrait with Model* by Ernst Ludwig Kirchner (1880–1938). *Kunsthalle, Hamburg.*

While Matisse wanted his pictures to be joyful, many of the Scandinavian and German artists known as expressionists were more interested in violent or unhappy feelings. They painted a great many self-portraits, staring into a mirror and out of the picture, trying to explore their most extreme states of mind.

In earlier times people were less interested in what artists were feeling. Artists were just expected to use their skills to do their job. But, during the romantic period of art, in the nineteenth century, people began to think of artists (including poets and composers) as able to express feelings better than other people.

In Germany, a number of artists formed a group known as Die Brücke (The Bridge). They included Ernst Ludwig Kirchner, Erich Heckel (1883–1970), and Karl Schmidt-Rottluff (1884–1976). They valued truthfulness more than clever techniques, and, in fact, they often used deliberately rough ways of working, as if that were a proof of the strength of their feelings. Their interest in simple, direct expression made them enthusiastic about the kind of art they called "primitive." This included work from almost every society outside Europe as well as peasant art from their own countries, but it was African art that had the most influence on them.

Primitivism

Primitive originally just meant from early times. When European explorers began to travel around the world in the fifteenth and sixteenth centuries, they found countries with cultures different from their own. They decided they must be less developed, even those cultures that were thousands of years old. When the Europeans wanted to take the resources of these countries, they claimed that they were bringing progress. Objects from these countries, however beautiful, were brought back to Europe as curiosities and put in museums to show how "uncivilized" their makers were. At the beginning of the twentieth century, some European artists came to admire and copy the style, sometimes called primitivism, of these curiosities. The word is also used to describe a preference for simplicity in any period.

Right A Bakongo tribal mask from Africa. Masks like this, which apparently possessed a ritual power because they were used in religious ceremonies, fascinated many artists at the beginning of the twentieth century, including Pablo Picasso (see page 14).

By 1900, some people were beginning to believe that modern civilization had become too artificial and that human beings, crowded into cities, had lost touch with their true nature. From this point of view, societies that appeared to be less complicated looked more attractive. The unusual objects in museums, such as tribal masks and carved figures, seemed mysterious and exciting to artists who wanted to make powerful art themselves. Knowing very little about the people who had made these

things, or what these things were for, European artists imagined whatever suited their own ideas.

Children who are frightened by their own anger often imagine "scary monsters." Adults also sometimes deal with complicated feelings by imagining they belong to someone else or to someplace outside themselves. Expressionist artists often felt the world was unhappy and confused. The idea of the primitive gave them a

Self-Portrait with Irises by Paula Modersohn-Becker (1876–1907). This serious, self-questioning image contrasts with Kirchner's spiky self-portrait on page 9. Disturbed by women's new independence, many male artists in the early 1900s portrayed themselves as powerful, even brutal figures. Women artists had to overcome the myth of the "macho genius." *Private collection.*

safe place to explore these strong feelings away from the realities of modern life.

At the end of the nineteenth century a similar impulse had led Paul Gauguin to leave France and go to work in Tahiti and the Marquesas Islands in the Pacific Ocean. Many of the expressionists admired Gauguin's work, and because they usually lived in cities, they were attracted by the idea of going back to nature, to the "other" world of peasant life in the country.

In the same way, because most of them were men, expressionist artists saw women as "the Other." Many of their pictures show women as mysterious creatures, sometimes weak, sometimes threatening, but always less civilized and closer to nature than men. Of course, these images had nothing to do with real women. Many women artists of the time, such as Paula Modersohn-Becker, struggled to resolve the contradictions between their own lives and the ideas they shared with expressionism.

Composition by Wassily Kandinsky (1866–1944). Musical titles encourage people to think about the general mood the painter is trying to create. But the picture's other title – *Cossacks* – prompts them to find the soldiers on the right-hand side. The cossacks have red hats and long bayonets. *Tate Gallery, London.*

The search for more powerful means of expression went deeper than simply borrowing primitive subjects and techniques. Toward the end of the nineteenth century, Gauguin and the symbolists had already begun to explore how a picture could create mood through the use of shape and color rather than through what people thought about the subject.

There was a lot of discussion about whether painting should stop imitating the appearance of things and become more abstract, like music. Music does not usually copy anything but it can still make people feel very strongly – happy or sad, excited or peaceful.

Wassily Kandinsky, a Russian artist who worked in Germany, used the bright colors and patterns of Russian folk art in his early work. He was especially interested in the connection between music and pictures because he often "saw" certain colors in his head when he heard

The Purple Fox by Franz Marc (1880–1916). Marc thought animals were nobler than humans, and he tried to imagine how nature would seem through the eyes of an eagle or a dog. He believed colors had symbolic meanings: blue was spiritual; red, heavy and brutal; yellow, gentle and cheerful. *Heydr Museum, Wuppertal, Germany.*

particular sounds. He also said that he could "hear" colors. This may seem an odd suggestion, but people quite often use words that describe sounds to say something about what they see – they talk, for example, of "loud" colors or colors that "clash."

In 1911, Kandinsky and Franz Marc founded a group called Der Blaue Reiter (Blue Rider). They published a book showing work by modern artists alongside primitive and folk art and children's drawings. Kandinsky believed that art should be about spiritual beliefs rather than surface appearances. Catching sight of one of his pictures lying upside down in the half-light one evening, Kandinsky was convinced that the abstract qualities of a painting were more important than the subject. For a few more years, however, Kandinsky still used the outer world as a starting point for his paintings.

4 CUBISM AND AFTER

Left *Les Demoiselles d'Avignon (The Girls of Avignon)* by Pablo Picasso (1881-1973). This painting made people question the "pin-up" poses found in Academic paintings of nude women, because it showed them with faces borrowed from Iberian sculpture and African masks, similar to the one on page 10. *Museum of Modern Art, New York.*

Right *Still Life with Fringing* by Picasso. The artist has played sophisticated games with space in this apparently simple construction. The wooden cup is hollow but its open end is solid and casts a real shadow, while the shadows on the moldings are painted. The fringe is a joke about gold frames on Old Master paintings. *Tate Gallery, London.*

When Pablo Picasso first showed Les Demoiselles d'Avignon to his friends in 1907, they hated it. The big "ugly" painting, with its cartoonlike faces, seemed to be deliberately making fun of everything they admired, including Picasso's own earlier work – gentle, rather sad pictures of circus people and beggars. The painting was not on public display until 1937.

Even today, after nearly 90 years, this is still a startling picture. The life-size figures, with their awkward bodies, glare blankly. Picasso, like the expressionists, was impressed by African masks, and they played a very big part in the development of this picture. But the painting is important to the history of modern art because of the way Picasso treated space.

Space in pictures is hard to talk about because, of course, it's not really there – it is an illusion. A traditional painting is like a model theater, with figures standing firmly on the floor, some of them close to the front of the stage while others might be toward the back. Picasso often went against the traditional rules of perspective and modeling—the way objects within a painting are shaped with paint to appear three dimensiomal. He chose to represent some normally unified surfaces as separate from the rest. For example,

Right *Clarinet and Bottle of Rum on a Mantelpiece* by Georges Braque (1882-1963). The fireplace at the bottom of the picture has a marble scroll supporting the mantelpiece. Everything seems to tilt in different directions. Look for the clarinet behind the bottle and the nail with its painted shadow. *Tate Gallery, London.*

in *Demoiselles d'Aviginon* a nose is a flat surface, a breast is a diamond-shaped surface, not continuous with the rest of the body. Also, the drapery surrounding the women is painted as a series of geometric shapes, not a flowing, loose piece of cloth such as the pink dress of the seated woman in *Friday at the Salon* (p.6).

The pictures that Picasso and his friend Georges Braque painted between 1907 and 1914 were called cubist, because a critic said that some of them looked as if they were made of little cubes. Some of the earliest ones were rocky landscapes but later Picasso and Braque tended to concentrate on their everyday surroundings, depicting objects in cafés or studios.

Some people say that cubist paintings show objects from several sides, but the effect is more like looking through a kaleidoscope, which breaks up the image into little pieces. Imagine a painter drawing a still life. Instead of standing back to get an overall view, imagine that she gets in close and draws each part almost as if she were touching it. These separate fragments won't necessarily join up in the imaginary space of the picture, but they could come together as a pattern of brushmarks on a flat surface.

Collage

Collage comes from the French word *coller,* meaning to glue. Gluing paper or other materials on to a flat surface to help make a picture is such a simple technique that it is astonishing how important it has been for the development of twentieth-century art. Cutting and gluing colored paper helped artists to think of pictures as arrangements of flat shapes. Images and photographs could also be put together to make political comments (see photomontage on page 22) or odd, dreamlike combinations (see pictures on pages 26–29). Transferred to three dimensions, collage also introduced the possibility of constructed sculpture. Today, collage is widely used in advertising and illustration.

Teacups by Juan Gris (1887–1927). Shading confuses the difference between flat pattern and illusions of depth. Gris has also included a private joke about cubism – a newspaper story about a new law banning poster-sticking ("collage" or gluing) on public monuments. *Kunstslig, Dusseldorf.*

Picasso and Braque stopped using bright color for a while because they wanted to concentrate on drawing. It is important to remember that they were not trying to make abstract paintings but wanted to find new ways of drawing objects in space. To make sure that the subject did not disappear completely from their pictures, they would put in little clues – more carefully painted details such as violin strings or buttons or letters. Most cubist paintings have clues in them. Often the title of a painting will help you look for these clues. At this time they were not showing their work at the Salons but were painting just for themselves and a few other people, so it did not matter if others understood their pictures.

After a while, Picasso and Braque began to think that it would make sense to replace the details with the real thing. What was the point of carefully painting a label on a bottle when you could stick the actual label right on the picture? They liked this reminder that pictures are real, solid objects, just like anything else in the world. They began to use pieces of newspaper, chopping headlines to make jokes and puns, and mixing news items into pictures of their everyday surroundings. This technique is known as collage, and when Picasso and Braque began to use it, it was taken up by the third major cubist painter, Juan Gris.

Once people began gluing things onto a picture, it was a small step to make constructions more three-dimensional using larger and more varied objects. Picasso started to construct small models of the guitars and wineglasses he featured in his paintings, first

Right *Homage to Blériot* by Robert Delaunay (1885–1941). This painting celebrated the first airplane flight over the English Channel. Look for the Eiffel Tower and the plane's propeller. *Musée d'Art Moderne, Paris.*

Below *Sleeping Muse* by Constantin Brancusi (1876–1957). The first version of this was carved in marble, the features barely breaking the hard surface. Here it is cast in bronze and polished to a smooth sheen. *Metropolitan Museum of Art, New York.*

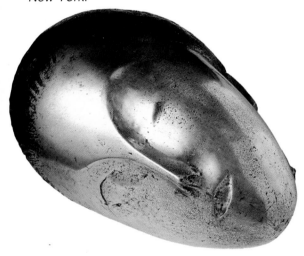

from folded paper and cardboard, and later in metal or wood. He probably did not think of them as sculpture at first. Sculpture had traditionally been made by modeling a figure (usually in clay, to be cast in metal), or carving into stone or wood. Auguste Rodin (1840–1917) had already begun to change sculpture from something suitable for monumental statues of important people to a much more lively and experimental medium.

Constantin Brancusi, who had arrived in Paris in 1904, was beginning to explore the medium of carved and polished marble, alongside the rich wood-carving tradition of his native Romania. Now, alongside the other approaches, cubist constructions suggested a third and extremely productive way of thinking about sculpture.

Many artists passed through a cubist phase before moving on in a different direction. Unlike some of the artists in the last chapter, many found life in a modern city like Paris very exciting. They enjoyed the crowds and cars and the babble of information from posters, newspapers, and conversations overheard in the street. The broken-up quality of cubist painting and collage seemed a good way to show all this excitement in pictures.

Artists (the futurists in Italy and Orphists in France) celebrated modern machines and the speed of planes and racing cars. Orphists Robert Delaunay and his wife Sonia Delaunay (1884–1979) (see page 25) painted scenes of Paris and the effects of light, using bright colors like those in the work of Matisse and Kandinsky.

5 ARTISTS AND THE WAR

The Menin Road by Paul Nash. The jagged pattern of lines increases the effect of this nightmare landscape of mud and debris, the result of four years of trench warfare during the World War I. *Imperial War Museum, London.*

Many of the newspapers used in the cubist collages of 1912 refer to fighting in eastern Europe, which a lot of people were worried about at that time. By 1914, this conflict had developed into something much bigger – World War I, which continued until 1918. The effects of the war were enormous. So many soldiers were killed or injured that it seemed as though a whole generation of young men had been destroyed. The war also destroyed people's confidence in ideas of progress. Scientific invention, instead of helping people, was being used to make more effective weapons. Although soldiers on both sides started out believing they were fighting for a good cause, by 1916 many felt that the politicians and the generals were continuing the war pointlessly.

Some artists tried to show people back home what the battlefields were really like. Others tried to avoid the war altogether. A small group of artists from several different countries ended up in Zurich, Switzerland, which was not involved in the conflict.

In 1916, the group started a combined club and art gallery called the Cabaret Voltaire. The name they chose for their activities was dada – a nonsense word, a child's first sounds. If the

The Forest by Jean Arp (1887–1966). This wooden relief looks simple, almost innocent, as if Arp were deliberately avoiding the world of war and machines. *National Gallery of Art, Washington.*

The Bride Stripped Bare by her Bachelors. Even (The Large Glass) by Marcel Duchamp (1887–1968). This unfinished artwork was smashed on its way to an exhibition. Duchamp spent months piecing it together, pleased that an accident had finally completed the work. *Philadelphia Museum of Art, Philadelphia.*

supposedly sensible, adult world had led to the madness of war, then they didn't want to belong to it.

They also wanted to avoid making the kind of art that would end up in museums or on the walls of houses of the rich people, whom they blamed for the war. So they made masks and puppets and, as the futurists had done, performed noise music and nonsense poetry. Alsace-born artist Jean Arp wrote later, "While the thunder of the guns rumbled in the distance, we pasted, we recited . . . we sang with all our soul . . . (to) save mankind from the madness of those times."

In New York, the name dada was adopted by another group of artists, including the Frenchmen Marcel Duchamp and Francis Picabia (1879–1953), and the American Man Ray (1890–1977). They were less concerned about the war and society, but used humor to question traditional ideas about art. Marcel Duchamp took ordinary objects, slightly altered or given a title, and exhibited them as "ready-mades." He was not claiming that these objects were particularly beautiful – in fact he deliberately tried to avoid letting his taste affect his choice – but he wanted people to think about the assumptions they make when they decide whether something is art or not.

6 ART AND THE RUSSIAN REVOLUTION

The Golden Cockerel by Natalia Gontcharova (1881–1962). This stage design for the Russian Ballet mixes folk art and cubism. *Private collection.*

Before World War I, artists of all nationalities came to work in the major European cities. Magazines and exhibitions of modern art spread the new ideas from one country to another. Russia was part of this international movement. Some Russian artists, such as Kandinsky, went to work abroad, while rich merchants in Moscow and St. Petersburg were important early collectors of work by Picasso and Matisse.

At the time, there was a revival of interest in traditional Russian folk art. For foreigners this was just another kind of exotic, primitive art.

The Russian Ballet, for example, had a big success in Paris with such works as Stravinsky's *The Firebird* and *Petrushka*. But for Russian artists, peasant art was also a way of rediscovering a sense of national identity and pride. (Similar feelings were emerging all over Europe. Nationalism could be a source of pride – but it also helped to cause World War I.)

Kasimir Malevich (1878–1935), in his early work, combined these Russian themes with a form of cubism. But unlike the cubists, and like Kandinsky (see page 12), he believed that art should express the invisible, spiritual world

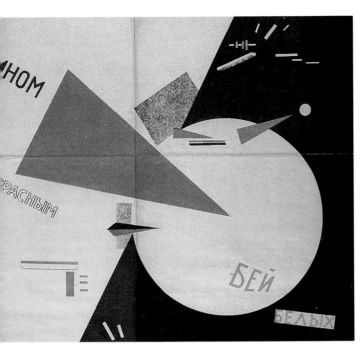

Beat the Whites with the Red Wedge. This poster by El Lissitsky (1890–1941) describes the struggle between Red (revolutionary) forces and White (czarist) forces. Magazines today still show the influence of the Russian's use of bold colors and lettering. *Private collection.*

Architectonic Composition by Liubov Popova (1889–1924). This energetic work seems to reflect the excitement felt by many about the Russian Revolution. *Leonard Hutton Galleries, New York.*

and that it could not do that if it was tied to the real world. In 1915, he exhibited his first completely abstract painting, a black square on a white background. It was hung across the corner of the room, the traditional place for Russian icons (religious paintings).

When the Russian Revolution swept away the old rule of the czars in 1917, the younger artists were enthusiastic. They wanted to help build the new communist society in which everybody would be equal. Most of them agreed that the visual language that was appropriate for this new world was not the traditional art of the academies but the new abstract art, with simple geometric shapes that everyone could understand. Over the next few years, while Russia struggled through civil war, food shortages, and foreign invasion, some people came to believe that art should have a practical use. Vladimir Tatlin (1885–1953), Liubov Popova, and Varvara Stepanova (1894–1958), among others, wanted to be more like engineers than artists, using their knowledge of materials, visual skills, and inventiveness to design industrial goods and posters, books, and textiles, which would be of immediate use in everyday life. Film and

Priestess by Hannah Höch (1889–1978). Höch's dada photomontages mixed politics with an interest in images of women. Here she has used contrasts of light and dark, sight and touch, and repeated curves and scrolls to make a gentle, sensuous image. *Private collection.*

Photomontage

This is a kind of collage made from photographs. Early in the twentieth century in Berlin, artists such as Hannah Höch and Raoul Hausmann were bringing together separate images from newspapers, magazines, and advertising to make jokes or comments on current events or politics. Because photography was associated with the everyday world, these images could have more impact than paintings, especially when they were rephotographed to appear more believable. Later John Heartfield used this technique to campaign against the rise of Adolf Hitler and Fascism; he was eventually forced to leave Germany.

photography, because they represented technology and progress, were an important part of this new art known as constructivism.

In Germany, another group of artists was enthusiastic about constructivist ideas and also hoped to bring about political change. As World War I came to an end, the defeated Germans were hungry and disillusioned. Some artists turned to expressionism, with its stress on inner feelings, but this seemed like feeble escapism to Richard Huelsenbeck (1892–1974), who came back to Berlin in 1917 from Zurich full of excitement about the dada events there.

Huelsenbeck and his colleagues – who included George Grosz (1893–1959), John Heartfield (1891–1968), Raoul Hausmann (1886–1971), and Hannah Höch – adopted the name dada for their own movement. Dada in Berlin was more political than in other cities. Rather than making anti-art gestures to change the way people thought about art, the Berlin artists hoped to change society. George Grosz used his drawing skills to make savage caricatures of those people who had made a profit out of the war, but the most important medium of the Berlin dada artists was photomontage.

7 INTO THE TWENTIES – THE SEARCH FOR ORDER

The Mechanic by Fernand Léger (1881–1955). Léger admired the precision of modern machines and the skill of the workers who made them. Here he combined a clean-cut mechanical style with the solemn profile found in Egyptian art to produce a heroic but down-to-earth image of a modern working man. *National Gallery of Canada, Ottawa.*

We have seen how some artists turned away from the traditional values of society and of the businessmen and politicians they blamed for the war. A different way to cope with the horror of what had happened was to look for comforting images of peace and stability.

In France, pictures of mothers and babies became popular for a while, and some artists turned back to traditional styles. But critics also began to point out that certain types of modern art had something in common with the solid, carefully composed works of such seventeenth-century painters as Nicholas Poussin and Claude Lorraine. Looked at in this way, the work of Cézanne and later artists such as Fernand Léger could be seen as carrying on the classical tradition in French art – solid geometric figures in calm, balanced compositions.

Because of the dominance of shape and color in abstract art the artist is able to concentrate on images of balance and order. The Dutch painter Piet Mondrian shared with Kandinsky and Malevich the belief that art should deal with the spiritual side of life. His early work showed the Dutch landscape, its flatness

Composition by Piet Mondrian (1872–1944). From the mid 1920s, Mondrian used a limited range of colors and shapes. These patterns have come to stand for an idea of modernity, used in so many kinds of designs that the hand-painted subtlety of the originals can come as a surprise. Look at the careful spacing of the lines and the effect of leaving the black edges off some of the colored blocks. *Tate Gallery, London.*

broken by the vertical lines of trees or windmills; he used color in a heightened, symbolic way. Around 1910 he discovered cubism and for a while he worked in Paris, making a series of paintings that gradually simplified images of the real world into a pattern of straight lines. Back in Holland during World War I, he continued this process with a series called *Pier and Ocean*.

Mondrian believed that reality is based on a series of opposites: horizontal and vertical, dark and light, female and male. He believed the artist could help people toward spiritual truth by offering images of perfect balance, which could never be achieved in the everyday world. Even people who disagree completely with his views can be moved by the care with which Mondrian pursued his ideal. Using only primary colors (red, yellow, and blue) along with black and white, he would paint and repaint each picture until the balance seemed exactly right.

A group of artists and designers associated with Mondrian in Holland were known by the name of the magazine they published, De Stijl (Style). They used a similar range of clean, square shapes and primary colors, but were mainly interested in applying them to the design of architecture, furniture, magazines, and posters.

Left *They're Biting*, by Paul Klee (1879–1940). This tiny picture uses a combination of watercolor and drawing, which Klee described as "taking a line for a walk." His ideas about art combined a poetic imagination with an interest in order and form. *Tate Gallery, London.*

Below *Coat and Citroën Car.* Sonia Delaunay designed these for the Paris Exhibition of Decorative Arts (Art Deco). They show how developments in painting, such as *Homage to Blériot* (page 17), were absorbed into other areas of design. *Bibliothéque Nationale, Paris.*

The ideas common to the De Stijl group and the Russian constructivists were also encouraged by a new kind of art school, the Bauhaus, set up in Germany in 1919. Here, the search was for the most rational and functional architecture, design, and craftsmanship. Students were taught to investigate the basic elements of form and color by artists and designers from all over Europe, including Kandinsky, Paul Klee, and László Moholy-Nagy (1895–1946). In the practical workshops, they also learned the use of different materials and were eventually encouraged to design for industrial production. When Hitler came to power in Germany in 1933, the Bauhaus was forced to close and many of the staff fled to England and the United States. Even today, the influence of the Bauhaus is still strong in art education and in the design of many household objects.

All over Europe and the United States, similar work (the international modern style) was based on a belief that buildings, furniture, and domestic goods should be designed like cars or airplanes – to do their job simply and effectively, stripped of unnecessary ornament. The architect Le Corbusier (1887–1965) used this approach in his Pavilion of the New Spirit, designed for the 1925 International Exhibition of the Decorative Arts, and summed up in his statement, "a house is a machine for living in."

8 SURREALISM

Left *Head of a Catalan Peasant* by Joan Miró (1893–1983). The peasant's red cap and his beard are set in a faint grid pattern that brings to mind the flat surface of the canvas. One eye is smaller than the other, so the face looks as if it is turned to one side, while the clouds suggest a deep space, with the "eyes" as planets. *Private collection.*

Freud and the Subconscious
The writers and artists known as surrealists were interested in the research of the psychiatrist, Sigmund Freud (1856–1939), who suggested that people are only conscious of a small part of the human mind. The rest, hidden below the surface like an iceberg, he called the subconscious. This hidden world surfaces only when the conscious mind is not working; for example when a person is dreaming or not concentrating, or when some coincidental pattern in the world suddenly suggests an image.

Most of the postwar artists and designers discussed in the last chapter were trying to build a world where everything could be defined and organized sensibly and rationally. But there is another side to human beings – irrational, unplanned, subconscious. When a person doodles during class or a phone call, what is that person thinking about? Most often, it is not the drawing; the drawing seems to happen by itself. And when a person dreams, the subconscious surfaces, expressing itself in weird images and events.

Throughout history, different people have

Right *The Entire City* by Max Ernst (1891–1976). Scraping wet paint across a canvas laid over different textures suggested an image which Ernst then developed into a haunting vision of an abandoned city. *Kunsthaus, Zurich.*

linked art and creativity to the less conscious side of the mind. Leonardo da Vinci, in the fifteenth century, recommended that artists encourage their imaginations by staring at cracks and marks on walls. You may have found that drawings sometimes turn out better when you are not concentrating too hard.

The group of writers who, in 1924, first adopted the name surrealism, was led by the poet André Breton (1896–1966). They experimented with what they called automatic writing. They would try to go into a trancelike state so that they could talk or write without really thinking about what they were saying. They also used to play a game called "Consequences," in which each person would write a part of a sentence, then fold the paper to hide the words, and pass it on to the next person to continue writing. They hoped the results of these experiments would suggest marvelous new images as well as revealing the workings of their subconscious minds.

Painters were excited by the new freedom surrealism encouraged. The paintings by Joan Miró—sharp, bright pictures of his family farm in Spain, became inhabited by fantastic

Italian Square – Melancholy by Giorgio de Chirico (1888–1978). Long shadows and a suggestion of brooding silence give de Chirico's work a nightmare quality that was later copied in many Hollywood movies. *Christie's Gallery, London.*

creatures. He also experimented with a version of automatic writing by scrubbing paint thinly onto the canvas to suggest images. He wrote: "As I paint, the picture begins to suggest itself under my brush. The form becomes a sign for a woman or a bird as I work. The first stage is free, unconscious. But the second stage is carefully calculated."

Max Ernst (1891–1976) used a range of similar techniques. These included taking rubbings with paper and crayon from heavily textured materials such as grained wood or scraping paint away from canvas. Another surrealist technique involved squeezing paint between two sheets of paper, then peeling one sheet away. (This is often done in art classes with folded paper, which gives a symmetrical, butterfly-like image.)

Ernst also made collages using engraved illustrations cut from old catalogs, novels, and magazines that he put together in odd combinations to produce mysterious or

Above *Fur Breakfast* by Meret Oppenheim (b. 1913). Like other surrealist works, this disturbing version of a familiar object was designed to upset normal expectations – the idea of using this cup and saucer makes us feel uneasy. *Museum of Modern Art, New York.*

Right *The Human Condition* by René Magritte. Magritte made several versions of this theme, which reminds us that even the most convincing painted illusion is not real. Modern advertisements borrow many similar images from surrealism, to catch consumers attention.*Simon Spierer collection.*

disturbing images, quite unlike the original cubist use of the technique. A sculptural variation of this involved extraordinary mixes of objects, sometimes poetic, sometimes frightening or funny.

After the earlier period of automatic techniques in the 1920s, surrealist painting shifted toward the realistic depiction of dreamlike scenes. The Italian artist Giorgio de Chirico had explored similar themes before World War I, and his work was much admired by the surrealists and served as an inspiration to many of them.

Other painters of these "dream postcards" included Salvador Dali (1904–89), whose well-known pictures of soft watches are less surrealist (surreal) than the movies he made with the film director Luis Buñuel. The paintings of the Belgian René Magritte (1898–1967) are more truly dreamlike, perhaps because they are of ordinary people or places that just happen to have something unusual about them.

9 REALISM IN THE THIRTIES

Tarasco Civilization – Fabric Dyeing by Diego Rivera (1886–1957). Rivera had been a cubist painter in Paris where he knew Picasso. After his return to Mexico, he used a mixture of modern and traditional styles in large wall paintings, telling the story of Mexican civilization. *National Palace, Mexico City.*

By the beginning of the 1930s, several groups of artists besides the surrealists were reviving more conventional, realistic styles of painting, for many different reasons.

Traditional styles of representation do not usually draw attention to the artist's point of view or to how the image was constructed, so whatever is shown seems natural. In the 1930s, Adolf Hitler and Josef Stalin, both political dictators, encouraged the use of this kind of realism for their official propaganda art because it made things seem true without people realizing they were being persuaded.

Realism

Realism is not as straightforward a word as it seems to be. It is easier to think about realistic art if is compared to photography. If an artist were going to take a photograph of a factory, she could stand a long way away so the factory seems to blend in to its surroundings, or she could come in close so the building looms up against the sky. The artist could show the factory workers looking relaxed, overworked, or proud of their achievements. If the artist were concerned about the environment, she might want to show pollution of local rivers, whereas the factory owners would probably choose a prettier, more positive view for their advertisements. All these photographs would be realistic but they would show different aspects of reality.

American Gothic by Grant Wood (1892–1942). It is easy to miss the careful staging of this famous image. At a time of terrible unemployment, Wood celebrated the values of rural small-town America in a dry, plain style that was part of his message. *Art Institute of Chicago.*

People who wanted to fight this kind of propaganda disagreed on the best method of protest. Some wanted to use the old familiar styles because they were popular. Others felt that because life was changing, old techniques of spreading information could not represent reality well enough.

German playwright Bertolt Brecht (1898–1956) believed that artists and writers should not use the same tricks, even for a good cause. Instead, they should help the audience think for themselves by deliberately using techniques that would remind them that they were seeing something artificial. He said, "I do not want

members of the audience to hang their brains up with their overcoats."

But whatever the original intentions of modern art, the fact was that a lot of people still found it pointless or hard to understand. The world was in the middle of an economic depression with millions of people jobless and hungry; events in Europe were heading toward war again. Some artists began to wonder whether they should abandon the new ways of working and deal with these large human issues in a more straightforward way.

In Mexico, Diego Rivera, José Clemente Orozco (1883–1949), and David Alfara Siqueiros (1896–1974) were helping to establish a new democratic regime, telling the story of the

Guernica by Pablo Picasso. This huge mural was painted after the town of Guernica was destroyed by German bombers, supporting General Francisco Franco's Fascist army during the Spanish Civil War (1936–39). It was the first time that air power had been used to kill civilians, including women and children. The painting was displayed in the Spanish Pavilion at the Paris World Fair in 1937, just two months after the bombing. Picasso used no color, just black, white, and gray (perhaps to remind people of newsprint), and he also included echoes of earlier war paintings. Although some people felt that a more realistic style would better influence public opinion over this atrocity, the work had a huge impact. *Prado, Madrid, Spain.*

Mexican people in massive wall paintings (see page 30). These combined elements of the ancient Aztec and Mayan civilizations with other styles, including Roman frescoes, Renaissance figure paintings, and modern art. Another Mexican artist, Frida Kahlo (1907–54), drew on traditional styles for more personal work that was greatly admired by the European surrealists.

In the United States (as part of the New Deal to help the unemployed), many artists were commissioned to paint public murals. Many of them used the example of the Mexican artists to develop a popular, realistic style. There was also a deliberate move away from modern European styles in favor of plain, "no-nonsense" paintings celebrating a rural American lifestyle.

10 ABSTRACT EXPRESSIONISM

Left *Moon Woman* by Jackson Pollock (1912–1956). The title refers to a Native American legend, but the rhythmic pattern of the paint is as important as the image. In his most famous works, Pollock laid the canvas on the floor and dripped the paint in delicate webs of color. *Museum of Modern Art, New York.*

Painters and sculptors can work almost anywhere. But they also need to be where they can discuss their work with other artists, get it shown and talked about, and find people to buy it. In this century, most major cities have had some kind of network of galleries, collectors, and critics. Just as Hollywood became the center of the movie industry, Paris was the center of the professional art world until World War II (1939–45). Many artists and dealers then left Europe for the United States, and attention gradually shifted to New York City.

At this time, most younger American artists were influenced by Europeans such as Picasso, Matisse, Miró, and Léger, whose work they knew through magazines and exhibitions. Many of them had been involved with public art projects, which had helped give them some professional confidence. Like other artists at that time, they felt that art should deal with

Left *Waterfall* by Arshile Gorky (1904–1948). Gorky's late work combined a very physical use of paint with delicate line drawings, derived from landscape or human figures. *Tate Gallery, London.*

Right *Woman I*, by Willem de Kooning (1904–1989). De Kooning's abstract work of the 1940s developed from drawings of the human figure, cut up and overlaid with heavy, apparently random paint marks. His *Woman* series brings back the whole figure, but with savage humor. *Museum of Modern Art, New York.*

human subject matter, and that purely geometric abstract art had become cold and empty without the idealism of Mondrian's generation.

Picasso's *Guernica* (see pages 32–33) offered a different kind of model, and several Americans were painting works with partly abstract figures in a shallow, cubist-type space. Surrealist ideas about the unconscious mind encouraged Arshile Gorky to use memories of his childhood in Armenia to make a series of loose, almost doodling paintings.

During the 1940s, artists began to take more interest in the actual process of painting. There was widespread interest in the notion that, like handwriting, the kind of marks you make with paint can show the painter's state of mind. Some artists also compared the act of painting to the rituals of certain Native American peoples, such as sand paintings of the Navajo.

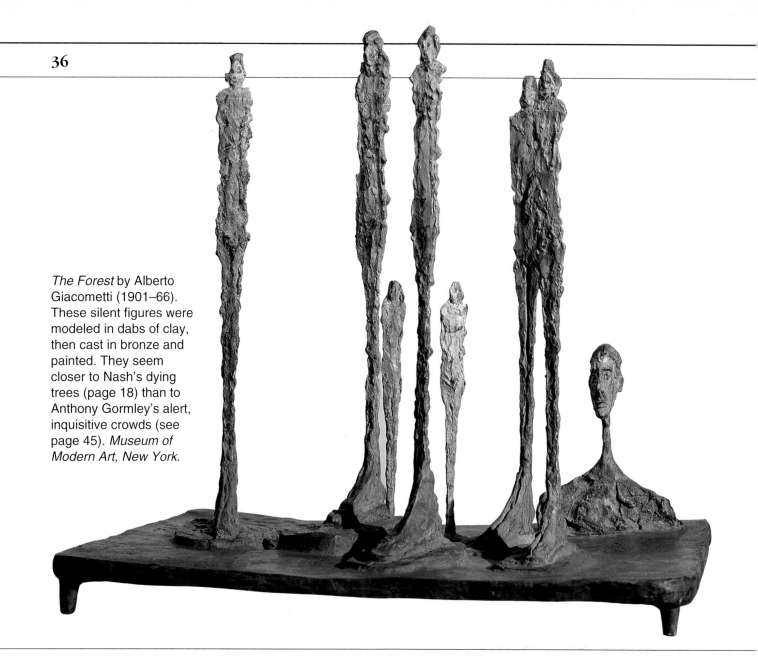

The Forest by Alberto Giacometti (1901–66). These silent figures were modeled in dabs of clay, then cast in bronze and painted. They seem closer to Nash's dying trees (page 18) than to Anthony Gormley's alert, inquisitive crowds (see page 45). *Museum of Modern Art, New York.*

Critics often emphasized the unplanned and energetic way that paintings were made and pointed out similarities to the way that jazz musicians use improvisation.

A group of New York painters, including Jackson Pollock, Barnett Newman (1905–70), Dutchman Willem de Kooning, and Russian-born Mark Rothko (1903–70), became known as the abstract expressionists. Their paintings look very different from one another but the painters shared certain beliefs about what art should be.

After the explosion of the first atomic bomb in 1945, at the end of World War II, human life seemed insignificant to a great many people in the face of a huge, empty universe. Any form of self-expression was a heroic act of defiance – an insistence that human beings do matter. In Europe, a similar mood was expressed through paintings or sculptures of the human figure, but the abstract expressionists believed that an abstract (but not impersonal) art could reach deeper levels of feeling.

The wish to turn personal feelings into grand statements may be one reason why they began to make large paintings. When you look at tiny reproductions in a book like this, it is easy to forget what a great impact enormously large paintings can have.

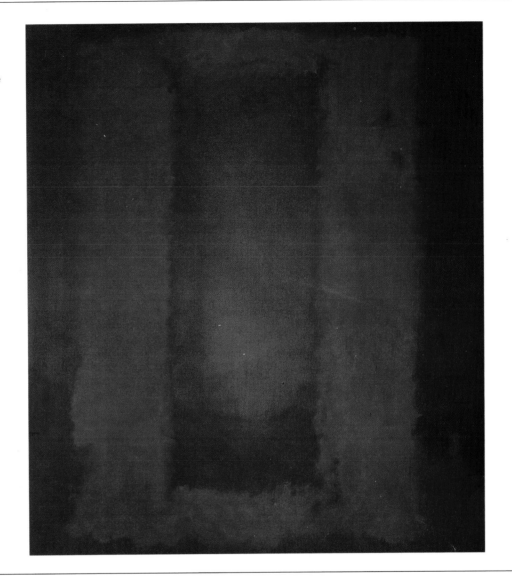

Red on Maroon by Mark Rothko. Photographs cannot convey the impact of Rothko's works and the subtle way the colors smolder against one another. In real life, these works are like giant doorways floating in space, pulling the spectator into their "magnetic" field. Rothko had been involved in experimental theater and wanted his paintings to work like abstract dramas, drawing people in emotionally and physically. *Tate Gallery, London.*

When a painting is taller than a person and stretches sideways farther than can be seen in one glance, people will look at it differently. Rather than looking into the picture as if the surface were a window, people are invited to explore it, just as they would a room they could stand in. The audience becomes much more involved in the painting. Many paintings by Jackson Pollock and Barnett Newman have this effect, which you can also experience with Claude Monet's large impressionist paintings of water lilies, which were painted many years earlier.

When they were younger, these New York artists had felt like outsiders. All the important living artists seemed to be on the other side of the Atlantic, and at home modern art was disliked and sneered at as a dangerous, possibly communist, foreign invention. Very soon after the war, however, the abstract expressionists began to achieve some success. By the middle of the 1950s, New York had become the center of the art world, and the United States government was sending exhibitions of American artist's work around the world as a display of American freedom. Now abstract expressionism had become the official art, and all the heroic talk was beginning to sound overblown to a new generation. Once again, it was time for something different.

11 POP ART AND THE SIXTIES

Just what is it that makes today's homes so different, so appealing? by Richard Hamilton (b.1922). This little collage is made from advertisements for the new consumer goods and popular entertainments of the 1950s. *Collection of Edwin Janss Jr, California.*

For more than a hundred years, the way that art has been displayed and discussed has tended to take it away from everyday life and into museums, encouraging the idea that people need special knowledge to understand and appreciate it. Some people have welcomed this separateness because it gives artists more freedom to experiment.

Others have tried to make art connect with daily life by including images from so-called popular culture – the ordinary and everyday, things that usually get left out of official views of "serious" art. Post impressionist pictures of circuses and cubist newspaper collages are examples – but they now hang respectably in museums.

In the 1950s, British artists, brought up in a gray postwar world, had a rather romantic view of American popular culture – Hollywood movies, rock' n' roll music, and glamorous, glossy cars. In 1956, a group of British artists organized an exhibition called This is Tomorrow. The artist Richard Hamilton argued that modern art should not be pompous, but young, witty, and fun. This view was shared by a number of younger artists, including Peter Blake (b. 1932) and David Hockney (b. 1937), at that time students at the Royal College of Art in London.

American artists had a slightly different attitude. Claes Oldenburg (b. 1929) celebrated the sheer messiness of New York street life.

Left *Retroactive II* by Robert Rauschenberg (b.1925). New printing techniques enabled Rauschenberg to mix newspaper images, reproductions of famous paintings and hand-painted areas of color. *Collection of Stefan T. Edlis.*

Above *Marilyn Monroe* by Andy Warhol (1928–1987). Warhol's images of the Hollywood star explore the fascination of fame and the way that repetition eventually leaves people feeling bored. (Viewed during the inauguration of the Warhol system, Paris 1990.)

Jasper Johns (b. 1930) produced images of the American flag with heavily worked, almost expressionist paint surfaces, while his colleague Robert Rauschenberg used photography and silk-screen printing to make densely layered images that to many people resemble dada collages.

Many other American pop artists preferred the impersonal feel of advertising and other mass-produced imagery. After all the emotional language used about abstract expressionism, the younger generation wanted to be cool and impassive. Instead of expressing inner feelings or observations from nature, they made secondhand images – pictures of pictures. Roy Lichtenstein (b. 1923) copied the machine-printed look of comic strips, while Andy Warhol took news photos, pictures of soup cans, or movie stars and repeated them over and over again. This apparently mindless repetition prompted questions about Warhol's intentions. Was he making a point about the way that newspapers and TV bombard people with images so relentlessly that they stop thinking about what they mean? Why should the meaning of a work depend on knowing what the artist thought? Was the whole point of the work to make people think about these kinds of questions?

These are complicated issues, but pop art appealed to people for its easily recognized subject matter and its bright colors, which

seemed to echo what was happening in fashion and popular music as well.

The idea that teenagers were a special group with their own tastes in clothes and music and a group of consumers to reckon with surfaced in the mid–1950s, with cinema idols like James Dean and rock stars like Elvis Presley. By the early 1960s, youth culture included miniskirts and the Beatles. A lot of the new art, like fashion and advertising, was bright, brash, and shiny.

Several American and British sculptors, such as David Smith and Anthony Caro (b. 1924), were making large pieces, in polished or painted metal, that seemed to make few references to natural forms. Others were exploring the possibilities of new materials such as fiberglass and plastic.

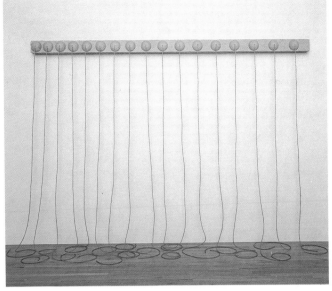

Above *Addendum* by American artist Eva Hesse (1936–1970). The logical, repetitive structures of minimal art become illogical and absurd in Hesse's work. Here the mathematical spacing of the gray domes is undermined by the rubber tubing that droops randomly onto the floor. *Tate Gallery, London.*

Above *Cubi XVIII* by David Smith (1906–1965). Smith ground his steel surfaces to catch the light, so that the solid volumes seem to balance almost weightlessly in the sunshine. *Private collection.*

Left *Hyena Stomp* by Frank Stella (b.1936). A simple geometric pattern, taller than a man, produces unexpected illusions of space. Stella later produced relief sculptures that push exuberantly off the wall and back into real space. *Tate Gallery, London.*

American Frank Stella was one of several painters making pictures that seemed to be about nothing other than themselves – repeated patterns painted in metallic or synthetic colors. He refused to let people read any kind of expressionist meaning into these works, saying "What you see is what you see." The taste for simplicity and repetition was shared by those artists (mainly sculptors) whose work is known as minimal art.

Minimal Art

Minimal art is work that uses very simple repeated shapes. Whereas earlier twentieth-century sculpture was often intended to be seen outdoors, minimal sculpture usually needed to be seen in a gallery space. Its critics claimed that if it wasn't shown in a gallery, you would never guess that it was supposed to be art. In fact, these works often have a very powerful presence in real life. As the sculptor Robert Morris (b. 1931) said, "Simple shapes don't necessarily produce a simple experience." It is like listening to music with a strong, simple beat. Sharing the enclosed space of a gallery with these orderly structures draws attention to the difference between the way people perceive things with their bodies and with their minds. As they move around them, the pattern they know stays the same while the pattern they see is constantly changing.

12 THE LAST 25 YEARS

Left *Balanced Slates* by British sculptor Andy Goldsworthy (b. 1956). Goldsworthy is interested in movement, change, growth, and decay and has worked with materials as fragile and short-lived as leaves and snow. Here, in the Lake District of England, a temporary balance has been achieved.

Over the last quarter of a century, many artists have challenged the idea (strongly argued by several critics in the 1960s) that art should be a specialist activity, to be judged only on its own terms – painting, for instance, only being "about" color, flatness, and shape. Although this view produced some powerful work (just as scientific progress often comes from people exploring ideas for their own sake rather than to solve specific problems), it also led to much undemanding and "tasteful" art, rather like background music.

During the 1960s, many artists were involved in the civil rights movement, the women's movement, and in protests against the Vietnam War. They began to find that the "pure" view of art was being used as an excuse to ignore any work that raised these uncomfortable issues. In particular, many black and women artists wanted to make art that described their own experiences and to explore the ways that images (in advertising, for instance) encourage very limited, stereotyped views of different groups of people.

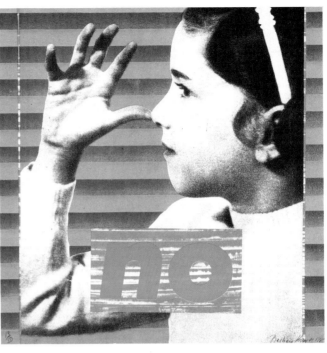

Above *Untitled* by American artist Barbara Kruger (b. 1945). Like Himid, Kruger uses humor to undermine accepted images, mixing photographs and captions in the glossy styles of magazines and posters. *Tate Gallery, London.*

Above *The Carrot Piece* by Lubaina Himid, who was born in Tanzania in 1954. She has described her work as " a mixture of humor, fury, celebration, and optimism. . . . I want to destroy the stereotypes that television, the newspapers, and advertisements are constantly feeding us [and show] black women as independent, strong-thinking people." *Private collection.*

There have been different ideas about what form such work should take. Some artists have felt the need to return to more traditional styles of painting or sculpture to reach a wider audience. Others believe that these complicated and important subjects need the widest possible range of approaches. These have included photography, writing, video and performance art – in addition to the richness and freedom of expression that painting and sculpture have acquired in the last hundred years.

During the late 1960s, some Minimal artists began to explore looser structures, where the making process was more important than the final shape, which was often a matter of chance. Using soft material, sewn or stacked or hanging, artists such as Eva Hesse produced works that were sometimes distorted, humorous echoes of the human body and sometimes more mysterious (see page 41).

The interest in process and unusual materials also took the form of so-called earth art, in

which artists used the landscape itself as their material. This coincided with the beginning of the environmental movement and a growing concern for the future of the natural world. However, many projects involved considerable interference with nature, such as *Spiral Jetty* by the American Robert Smithson (1938–73) or the work of Bulgarian-born Christo (b. 1935), who wrapped whole areas of coastline in cloth. Other work, such as that of Britain's Richard Long (b. 1945), was gentler. Because much of this work was temporary or sited in remote areas, most people knew it only through photographs and descriptions. It was often the

idea of the work that captured their imaginations.

Ideas, also communicated through photographs and writings, were the main point of conceptual art. Many conceptual artists were influenced by the work of Marcel Duchamp (see page 19) and his attempts to prod people into questioning the things they took for granted. German artist Joseph Beuys (1921–86) also had an enormous influence on younger artists, with work that cut across many different categories – lectures, performance, sculpture, and installations. His passionate belief that art

Above *The Dance* by Portuguese-born Paula Rego (b. 1935). Why are these solid figures dancing in the moonlight? The shadows they cast are not consistent, increasing the sense of mystery in this oddly tender scene. *Tate Gallery, London.*

Above *Field for the British Isles* by Britain's Anthony Gormley (b. 1950). Children from a local school worked with Gormley to produce the 40,000 little figures that crowd this room, staring up at the spectator. *Tate Gallery, Liverpool.*

Left *Dinner at West Hill* by English artist Howard Hodgkin (b. 1932). Hodgkin's pleasure in the brilliant color and pattern of Indian miniature painting is evident in this early example of his work. *Tate Gallery, London.*

has a social and political purpose was shared by many people.

The 1980s also saw plenty of revivals or parodies of earlier work, in art as well as fashion, movies, and television. Some people have taken this as proof that today's art has no original ideas of its own, but moves forward by "playing" with the past.

In spite of new technologies and all the alternative types of art, painting and sculpture have survived – figurative as well as abstract, expressionist as well as cool.

The exciting thing about the art being made right now is that people have not had time to create theories about it, or to define what is important. People make up their own minds about what they like, just as they choose what music to listen to. Many young artists now are concerned about the same sort of things as other people: bodies and feelings, how people relate to one another, and how they fit into the world. More people are approaching art with an open mind, accepting new styles, and accepting that art changes along with the people who create it and observe it.

GLOSSARY

Abstract Describes a painting that explores shapes, colors, and textures and shows them as satisfying in their own right, not as ways of depicting the real world. See *figurative*.

Academies Official schools where painters and sculptors were trained. By the nineteenth century these schools insisted on a style based on past art, and so *academic* has come to mean a fixed and old-fashioned approach to art.

Art deco (abbreviated from the 1925 Exhibition of Decorative Art) A style of decoration, jewelry, architecture, etc. The style was at its height in the 1930s.

Automatic Something done without conscious thought or effort.

Caricature An image of a person that exaggerates the person's features.

Classical Following the ideas originally expressed in the arts of ancient Greece and Rome, which emphasized simplicity, balance, and beauty.

Commissioned Art that is produced for a particular purpose or customer.

Communist Following the political ideas of communism.

Composition The arrangement of the various parts of a work, such as a painting or piece of music.

Construction A piece of sculpture made by joining separate parts together (such as by nailing or welding) rather than carving into wood or stone or modeling in a soft material such as plaster or clay.

Depression A long period of economic difficulty and unemployment, especially the period between 1929 and 1934 in the United States and Europe.

Fascism A system of government that controls everything in a country and that suppresses all public criticism or opposition.

Figurative Relating to the natural form or figure of things. The opposite of abstract art.

Functional Designed to be practical and useful rather than simply decorative.

Iberian Relating to the pre-Roman peoples of the peninsula that is now Spain and Portugal.

Impressionist The group of painters working in the latter half of the nineteenth century who concentrated on recording the effects of light and color.

Installation A work of art, such as a huge sculpture, through which spectators move.

Medium (plural: media) The material used to make a work of art.

Murals Large wall paintings.

Nationalism Pride in one's country, sometimes to the exclusion of people in other countries.

New Deal A government program in the United States in the mid-1930s designed to create jobs and end the Depression.

Parodies Works of art that mimic the style of others in a humorous way.

Performance art A work of art that is acted out in front of the audience, often by the artist.

Perspective A technique artists use to represent objects in space on a flat surface.

Popular culture The objects and art forms that are used and appreciated by the majority of people, rather than the more specialized forms of art.

Propaganda A publicity campaign that aims to persuade people to believe certain things or think in certain ways.

Rational Describes beliefs or ideas that are based on thought rather than on emotions or feelings.

Readymades A term used by Marcel Duchamp and others to describe everyday objects altered slightly and exhibited as if they were works of art.

Realistic In art, the effort to make a work of art represent the world as we see it.

Relief A work of art made in three dimensions, like sculpture, but designed to be set against a flat surface such as a wall and viewed from one side, like a painting.

Rubbings Images of objects with raised patterns or textures, such as coins or tree bark, that are made by rubbing chalk or crayon across a sheet of paper laid on top of the object.

Salon In France, an annual government-sponsored exhibition of art.

Spiritual Concerned with deeper or more religious aspects of life rather than physical or material things.

Stereotype A description that gives the same characteristics to a whole group of people and that denies the people any individual qualities.

Still life A painting or drawing of inanimate objects, such as flowers, fruit, books, etc.

Symbolic Using images or elements such as color to represent something else (such as an idea or feeling that cannot be shown directly).

Symbolists Artists painting at the end of the nineteenth century who incorporated symbolic meaning into their work. Also a poetry movement.
Women's movement The campaign (particularly in the 1960s and '70s) to change laws and people's attitudes to bring about equal rights for women.

FURTHER READING

American Heritage Illustrated History of of the United States, Vol. 13: World War I. Reprint of 1963 edition. Westbury, NY: Choice Pub NY, 1988.

Bohm-Duchen, Monica. *Understanding Modern Art.* Tulsa, OK: EDC Library Services, 1993.

Greenberg, Jan and Sandra Jordan. *The Sculptor's Eye: Looking at Contemporary American Art.* New York: Delacorte, 1993.

Janson, H. W. and Anthony F. Janson. *The History of Art for Young People.* 4th edition. New York: Harry N. Abrams, 1992.

Lyttle, Richard B. *Pablo Picasso: The Man and the Image.* New York: Atheneum, 1989.

Powell, Jillian. *Art in the Nineteenth Century.* Art and Artists. New York: Thomson Learning, 1995.

For older readers

Cole, Alison. *Perspective.* London: Dorling Kindersley, 1992.

Hughes, Robert. *The Shock of the New.* London: Thames and Hudson, 1991.

WHERE TO SEE MODERN ART

Boston
Museum of Fine Arts
465 Huntington Avenue
Boston, MA 02115
(617) 267-9300

Chicago
The Art Institute of Chicago
Michigan Avenue at Adams Street
Chicago, IL 60603
(312) 443-3600

Los Angeles
The Museum Of Contemporary Art
5905 Wilshire Boulevard
Los Angeles, CA 90036
(213) 857-6000

New York
The Museum of Modern Art
11 West 53rd Street
New York, NY 10019
(212) 708-9400

The Whitney Museum of American Art
945 Madison Avenue
New York, New York 10021
(212) 570-3600

Washington, DC
Hirschhorn Museum and Sculpture Garden
Smithsonian Institution
Independence Avenue at 7th Street, SW
Washington, DC 20560
(202) 357-3091

INDEX

Numbers in **bold** refer to illustrations